PRESENTED TO:

_____

FROM:

_____

Everything
TO God in
Prayer

Guided Prayers for Your
Deepest Needs & Biggest Dreams

DAVID JEREMIAH

CONTENTS

PRAYER FOR...

PRAYER FOR...

PRAYER FOR...

Rejoice always,
pray without ceasing,
in everything give thanks;
for this is the will of God
in Christ Jesus for you.

1 THESSALONIANS 5:16-18

INTRODUCTION

In a world constantly filled with uncertainty—political tensions, economic challenges, personal struggles—I've learned one transformative truth: Our destiny is not determined by circumstances but by our connection to God through prayer.

Throughout my years of ministry, I've witnessed numerous believers wrestling with life's difficulties, searching for hope and guidance. This book is born from those moments—from the intimate prayers shared at the end of my messages, from years of pastoral counseling, and from my own journey of learning to carry everything to God.

Prayer is not a last resort; it is our first and most powerful response. It's not about crafting perfect words but about opening our hearts honestly before a God who listens, understands, and responds. Each prayer in this collection emerges from real-life moments—moments of joy, pain, confusion, triumph, and hope—where I've sought divine wisdom and found supernatural peace.

You'll find these prayers arranged by topics and needs, designed to be both a model and a companion. They're not meant to replace your personal dialogue with God but to inspire and guide you into deeper, more confident communion with Him. Whether you're facing a momentous life challenge or wrestling with a seemingly mundane concern, these prayers remind you that no care is too small for God's attention.

The old hymn rings true: *O, what peace we often forfeit, O, what needless pain we bear, all because we do not carry everything to God in prayer.* We often forfeit peace and bear unnecessary pain simply because we fail to bring our concerns to our Heavenly Father. This book is an invitation—a roadmap—to transform that pattern. To learn that in Jesus, you have not just a distant deity but a friend who invites you into intimate conversation.

My prayer is that as you explore these pages, you'll discover a new freedom in prayer. I pray that you'll learn to approach His throne not with hesitation but with confident assurance, knowing that His love, mercy, and grace are always available—abundantly and unconditionally.

David Jeremiah

When I Am Waiting

KEY SCRIPTURE:

He gives power to the weak, and to those who have no might He increases strength. Even the youths shall faint and be weary, and the young men shall utterly fall, but those who wait on the Lord shall renew their strength; they shall mount up with wings like eagles, they shall run and not be weary, they shall walk and not faint.
ISAIAH 40:29-31

Heavenly Father,

Teach me how to wait. Teach me to understand that You will never disappoint me when I take You at Your Word and when I wait on You. I find great strength in our relationship.

Lord, I know what it's like to flap, but I know a little bit of what it's like to soar. And I want to spend the rest of my life soaring because I realize that's where the joy, the excitement, and the adventure really are.

Please kick me out of the nest. Help me not to find my joy in the comfort of security but in waiting upon You and walking with You every day.

In Jesus' Name, Amen.

When I Feel Stressed

KEY SCRIPTURE:

*Take my yoke upon you, and learn of me; for I am meek
and lowly in heart: and ye shall find rest unto your souls.*
MATTHEW 11:29, KJV

Heavenly Father,

May I discover afresh that my plans create stress and that Your plans are the only ones that work. Help me understand the reality of Your promise that I can find rest—not just for my body but also for my soul. Lord Jesus, I say "Yes" to Your offer of rest.

I let go of the yoke I've been carrying, and I let go of the stress that yoke has placed on my shoulders. I let go of everything that has been weighing me down and tripping me up. In its place, I take on Your yoke, my Savior, which I know is easy and light. I take up the yoke of living as Your disciple and following in Your ways.

I choose to lean on You, and I choose to learn from You.

In Jesus' Name, Amen.

PRAYER FOR...

When I Am
Worried
About Evil

KEY SCRIPTURE:

Do not fret because of evildoers, nor be envious of the workers of iniquity. For they shall soon be cut down like the grass, and wither as the green herb. Trust in the Lord, and do good; dwell in the land, and feed on His faithfulness.
PSALM 37:1-3

Heavenly Father,

I choose not to fret whenever I encounter evil in this world. Instead, I choose to trust.

Right now I'm asking to experience my faith-walk with You to such a degree that through trusting and delighting and committing, I will come to the place of resting. A place where no matter what may be happening in the world around me, no matter how difficult the problems surrounding me, I have a tremendous sense of trust that puts me at peace in heart and soul.

Lord, You are in control of all that happens here on earth and will judge the wicked. May I rest in these truths today, and may You bring peace to my heart and to those around me.

In Jesus' Name, Amen.

When I Feel Insecure or Anxious

KEY SCRIPTURE:

Be anxious for nothing, but in everything by prayer and supplication, with thanksgiving, let your requests be made known to God; and the peace of God, which surpasses all understanding, will guard your hearts and minds through Christ Jesus. Finally, brethren, whatever things are true, whatever things are noble, whatever things are just, whatever things are pure, whatever things are lovely, whatever things are of good report, if there is any virtue and if there is anything praiseworthy—meditate on these things.
PHILIPPIANS 4:6-8

Heavenly Father,

I'm grateful that I don't have to be anxious or insecure. Thank You that I don't have to settle for an anxiety-ridden, worry-driven life. That there's a better way to live, and You've spelled it out for me in Your precious Word. Take Your promises of peace and protection and drill them deep into my heart. Help me not to forget how much You love me. And, Lord, may I be bold enough and courageous enough to take these promises at their face value and put them into operation in my life. May my thoughts dwell solely on things that are true, noble, just, pure, and lovely.

In Jesus' Name, Amen.

When I Want to Be a Better Spouse

KEY SCRIPTURE:

Submit to one another out of reverence for Christ.
EPHESIANS 5:21, NIV

Father,

I hear Your Word instruct me and my spouse to submit to one another in our marriage, so I come before You asking for help. I know that submission is not weakness but strength and godliness.

Even so, I confess that it's difficult for me to submit to my spouse at times. My pride gets in the way. Therefore, please teach me to submit my will even as Christ submitted His will to You.

Sometimes I want to blame my spouse, but help me instead to be strong and godly, stepping forward to be the spouse You have called me to be. Give us both the grace to yield to one another out of our reverence for You.

And as we do, may our love for You and for each other grow even today.

In Jesus' Name, Amen.

When I Need Help in My Career

KEY SCRIPTURE:

Obey in all things your masters according to the flesh, not with eyeservice, as men-pleasers, but in sincerity of heart, fearing God.
COLOSSIANS 3:22

Dear Lord,

My work is a gift from You. My work is an opportunity to serve You, especially when I engage with those who may not know You. This is where real faith takes root.

So in the stress and strain of the marketplace, help me live a Spirit-filled life. Give me the power to be a faithful follower, living each day for the audience of One. Help me work as unto the Lord, knowing You see my every effort and will reward me according to what I have done.

Help me practice gratitude and grow in contentment so that I might be fulfilled in the work You've entrusted to me. And may my attitude and actions bring You glory and help others experience Your goodness.

In Jesus' Name, Amen.

When I Need Wisdom

KEY SCRIPTURE:

If any of you lacks wisdom, you should ask God, who gives generously to all without finding fault, and it will be given to you.
JAMES 1:5, NIV

Dear Lord,

Please give me Your wisdom. I confess that I lack wisdom, and I often feel an incredible sense of ignorance and confusion in my life. Even so, I take great hope and encouragement in this truth: You will always show me what I must do next. That's all I need to face this situation and make the right decision.

You have promised to give me all the wisdom I need for the moment and everything I need to take the next step. If I trust You and follow You today, I know You will prepare me for tomorrow.

I don't have to know the future because Your wisdom will be there as I walk in the light of today. So please, may I receive Your wisdom generously right now.

In Jesus' Name, Amen.

When I'm Concerned About My Children (Grandchildren)

KEY SCRIPTURE:

I am reminded of your sincere faith, which first lived in your grandmother Lois and in your mother Eunice and, I am persuaded, now lives in you also.
2 TIMOTHY 1:5, NIV

Father God,

Thank You for calling me to a ministry with my children (grandchildren). I say "Yes" to serving You by serving them. Like Lois and Eunice, may I demonstrate a sincere faith that will influence future generations with Your love.

Instill in me a faithfulness to Your Word that will grow in them, building a godly heritage of young men and women who delight in Your Word. Anoint me with a sense of the importance of this season, and may Your Holy Spirit quicken my mind to remember the truth of Your Word so that I can meet the situations of the day.

In the midst of stories, games, and time with my children (grandchildren), may they experience a safety net of love. And where there is brokenness in my family, I pray that You will take the Word of God and use it to bring healing and forgiveness. Bless Your truth to the hearts of my children (grandchildren) today.

In Jesus' Name, Amen.

PRAYER FOR...

When I Need
Courage

KEY SCRIPTURE:

I sought the Lord, and he answered me; he delivered me from all my fears. Those who look to him are radiant; their faces are never covered with shame. This poor man called, and the Lord heard him; he saved him out of all his troubles. The angel of the Lord encamps around those who fear him, and he delivers them.
PSALM 34:4-7, NIV

Dear Lord,

Thank You for drawing near to me. When I am afraid, You are my strength. And though I may not see You, I know You are here and You are enough. Nothing is too hard for You, and no one can stand against You.

When fear tries to creep in, help me remember how easy it is to take You off the throne of my life and put fear there instead. I renounce the fear that has taken over, for I know You hear me, even as You heard David in this psalm.

Help me worship not only in prosperity but also in the night of adversity, for You deliver me and You save me. All of my hope and strength is in You.

In Jesus' Name, Amen.

When I Feel Worthless

KEY SCRIPTURE:

Are not five sparrows sold for two copper coins? And not one of them is forgotten before God. But the very hairs of your head are all numbered. Do not fear therefore; you are of more value than many sparrows.
LUKE 12:6-7

Heavenly Father,

I thank You for the warm sense of Your smile over me. Thank You for all that I have because of what Jesus Christ has done on the cross. I am accepted forever.

You have loved me with an everlasting love. You know me, You're near me, You made me, and You're thinking of me. When I struggle with feelings of worthlessness, build me up on the inside with Your truth. May I rejoice that I am loved and cherished by my Savior.

When I look in the mirror and feel unworthy, help me look at my reflection in Your Holy Word, forever declaring that I am beautifully and wonderfully made. When I feel rejected, You call me Your very own. Encourage my heart with Your steadfast love.

I pray these things in Jesus' Name, Amen.

When I Need Peace

KEY SCRIPTURE:

Hear my cry, O God; attend to my prayer. From the end of the earth I will cry to You, when my heart is overwhelmed; lead me to the rock that is higher than I. For You have been a shelter for me, a strong tower from the enemy. I will abide in Your tabernacle forever; I will trust in the shelter of Your wings.
PSALM 61:1-4

Lord God,

There are so many things in my life that do not make sense. So I come now to the Rock that is higher than I. Help me accept that circumstances and people are not always fair.

I know You are just, and You never allow anything to happen in my life for which You do not have a purpose. Therefore, help me to walk triumphantly today because peace is Your promise to me; it is a result of Your work on the cross. Father, I need this nudge from Your Word to know that I'm okay because You shelter me when my heart is overwhelmed.

I pray for discipline and strength to exhibit true inner peace that goes beyond my understanding and that sustains me through the turmoil. Please be my shelter today, Heavenly Father. Please be my strong tower.

I pray this in Jesus' Name, Amen.

PRAYER FOR...

When I'm Battling Depression

KEY SCRIPTURE:

After this Job opened his mouth and cursed the day of his birth. And Job spoke, and said: "May the day perish on which I was born.... May that day be darkness; may God above not seek it, nor the light shine upon it."
JOB 3:1-4

Father God,

I am so thankful for the third chapter of Job. You revealed Job's story, including his depression, for a purpose—that I might understand how a person of great stature before You went through a dark night of the soul.

Just as You were with him, You are here with me. You sustain me. You will not forsake me. No matter the depths I experience, I will not lose my status before You.

Lord, hear my cry, bring me out of the miry clay, and set my feet upon the rock. You are my help and my deliverer. It is only through Your power that I can make it through these days.

I pray this in Jesus' Name, Amen.

When I Feel Lost

KEY SCRIPTURE:

Let us hear the conclusion of the whole matter: Fear God
and keep His commandments, for this is man's all.
ECCLESIASTES 12:13

Heavenly Father,

I confess that I can be easily knocked off track. I confess that I am often overwhelmed by situations and circumstances that feel huge to me but really are small in comparison to Your sovereignty.

Please help me return to the critical foundations mentioned by Solomon in this verse. First, please help me to fear You. I choose to fear You as almighty and all-powerful. I honor You, and I stand in awe of You. Second, please help me to keep Your commandments.

Please guide me according to Your will and Your Word each day, and please convict me whenever I disobey or wander from what You have declared to be right. Right now, please fill me with the joy and contentment that come from living each day in a close relationship with You.

In Your wonderful name, Jesus, Amen.

PRAYER FOR...

When I Struggle in Parenting

KEY SCRIPTURE:

Fathers, do not exasperate your children; instead, bring
them up in the training and instruction of the Lord.
EPHESIANS 6:4, NIV

Heavenly Father,

I know there are times when I have exasperated my children.
I confess every single time that has occurred. I repent of every
single time I have crossed a line by refusing to love them and serve
them as You do.

I know that if I follow Your truth, You will help me to obey You
with my whole heart. I pray that You will powerfully minister to
me and my children by Your Holy Spirit. Help me desire to do Your
will and be the best parent I can be for Your honor and glory and for
the benefit and health of my family.

I pray that our family might be strong and that we might build
second-generation believers. May Christ be exalted in all we do.

In Jesus' Name, Amen.

When I Need Hope

KEY SCRIPTURE:

*There I will give her back her vineyards, and will
make the Valley of Achor a door of hope.*
HOSEA 2:15, NIV

Dear Lord,

At times it seems like I have taken a side trip into the Valley of
Achor—the valley of trouble—and I've lost my hope. It's not Your
doing or the actions of someone else—perhaps I have inflicted
myself, and I feel stuck.

I know the enemy wants me to feel trapped, like there's no way
out. But You meet me in the valley, and You walk with me. I come to
You now, my steadfast hope. Thank You that I don't have to stay here,
for You lead me through the valley in peace.

Please fill me with hope. May I look in the mirror and see a
person looking back who has peace in their eyes.

In the name of my Savior, Amen.

PRAYER FOR...

When I Am Tempted

KEY SCRIPTURE:

Blessed is the man who endures temptation; for when he has been approved, he will receive the crown of life which the Lord has promised to those who love Him. Let no one say when he is tempted, "I am tempted by God"; for God cannot be tempted by evil, nor does He Himself tempt anyone.
JAMES 1:12-13

Dear Lord,

I pray that You would protect me when I face temptation. I know that every time there's a test, You provide a way out. Lord, I know how frail I am, but I want to be a person who endures.

I want to be approved by You. When I am tempted this week through a trial or challenge, please make me strong. Give me strength to be wise and to see the process the enemy uses to trip me up. And help me to fight, to follow You closely, and to flee from temptation.

Make me strong in Your Word so that I don't break down. Fill me with Your Spirit so that I overflow with strength to stand firm in the face of temptation. Help me see that in my own strength I cannot win, but in Your strength there is victory.

I pray this in Jesus' Name, Amen.

When I Need Courage to Share My Faith

KEY SCRIPTURE:

*Behold, I say to you, lift up your eyes and look at the
fields, for they are already white for harvest!*
JOHN 4:35

Heavenly Father,

I confess that I am often busy and distracted from seeing the
harvest all around me. Thank You for the privilege of sharing
the Gospel. In a world of bad news, help me to be faithful to my
calling of sharing the Good News.

I know there are people ready to be saved, living anxious and
busy lives. I believe that today is the day of salvation. Help me show
people Your goodness through my actions. Give me the courage
and power to share the story of Your sacrificial love anytime and
anywhere, regardless of the reaction.

Father, may I examine my life and prepare a story of what You've
done for me so that I can share it with those who may not know You.
May I never miss an opportunity.

In Jesus' Name, Amen.

PRAYER FOR...

When I Want a Stronger Marriage

KEY SCRIPTURE:

Wives, submit yourselves to your own husbands as you do to the Lord.... Husbands, love your wives, just as Christ loved the church and gave himself up for her to make her holy, cleansing her by the washing with water through the word, and to present her to himself as a radiant church, without stain or wrinkle or any other blemish, but holy and blameless.
EPHESIANS 5:22, 25–27, NIV

Dear Father,

May Your hand of blessing be upon my marriage today. When I fail to follow Your Word, my marriage can go on a downward cycle of conflict. Help me break that cycle through the power of Your love.

Give me the grace to surrender my will for the sake of my spouse and our marriage. Help me honor Your Word and fill me with a desire to follow Your commands, for in them I find freedom and rest.

Help me take initiative for the love and respect in my marriage. May I be willing to say "Yes" and do what You want me to do. May this obedience encourage my spouse and help our marriage grow stronger each day.

In Jesus' Name, Amen.

PRAYER FOR...

When I Want an Exuberant Faith

KEY SCRIPTURE:

*For not only has the word of the Lord sounded forth
from you in Macedonia and Achaia, but your faith in
God has gone forth everywhere, so that we need not say
anything. For they themselves report concerning us the
kind of reception we had among you, and how you turned
to God from idols to serve the living and true God, and to
wait for his Son from heaven, whom he raised from the
dead, Jesus who delivers us from the wrath to come.*
1 THESSALONIANS 1:8-10, ESV

Father,

Please teach me how to have a contagious faith.

Let it be through my lifestyle of exuberance that Your Word
sounds forth in my community and everywhere. May I live with
true, genuine, heartfelt enthusiasm. Let Your life in me boil out into
zeal and enthusiasm.

Lord, I want the Gospel to go forth everywhere. Instead of acting
like I'm in the Secret Service, help my faith shine like the sun with
You as my everlasting Light. Help my heart turn from idols so that I
serve You with a heart on fire. Let me leave an impression of grace
upon each person with whom I come in contact. And may all of this
be powered through Your Holy Spirit.

In the name of Jesus, Amen.

PRAYER FOR...

When I Feel
Unworthy

KEY SCRIPTURE:

When I consider your heavens, the work of your fingers, the moon and the stars, which you have set in place, what is mankind that you are mindful of them, human beings that you care for them? You have... crowned them with glory and honor. You made them rulers over the works of your hands; you put everything under their feet.
PSALM 8:3-6, NIV

My Good Father,

How wonderful is Your name in all the earth! The stars tell it, and little children understand it. But I confess that sometimes I miss it. Show me the wonder of what it means to be created a little lower than the angels. You have crowned me with glory and honor, and You care for me. Help me see each day as Your great opportunity, gladly giving in to Your design for my life.

You have made me for Yourself, to know Your goodness and display Your glory. May this truth be established deep in my heart. And help me to want to know You in such a way that every day will be a new discovery of who You are and how Your sovereignty works in my life. I give You all the praise.

In Jesus' Name, Amen.

PRAYER FOR...

When I Have
Feelings of Guilt

KEY SCRIPTURE:

I acknowledged my sin to You, and my iniquity I have not hidden. I said, "I will confess my transgressions to the Lord," and You forgave the iniquity of my sin.
PSALM 32:5

Father God,

Help me believe that no matter what, You will never stop loving me. There is hurt in my heart, and I feel out of sorts. I am bringing it all before You, not hiding anything.

I confess to You where I have been wrong. Thank You for being faithful to forgive me. I know it's impossible to get away with sin. Thank You that it's also impossible to get away from Your love.

You wait for me with wide-open arms and accept me as I come to You. Father, I pray also for those who were harmed by my words and actions. Cover with mercy what cannot be erased. And may Your grace be enough for every insufficiency.

In Jesus' Name I pray, Amen.

PRAYER FOR...

When I'm Not Growing in My Faith

KEY SCRIPTURE:

For our gospel did not come to you in word only, but also in power, and in the Holy Spirit and in much assurance, as you know what kind of men we were among you for your sake. And you became followers of us and of the Lord, having received the word in much affliction, with joy of the Holy Spirit, so that you became examples to all in Macedonia and Achaia who believe.
1 THESSALONIANS 1:5-7

Dear Father,

You have both called me and empowered me to grow as an example of Jesus Christ. Help me learn from believers through fellowship and the study of Your Word. Give me the grace to commit to relationships that not only inform me but also form me into the image of Your Son. I don't want to just mentally acknowledge Christian doctrine; I want full assurance of faith, growing each day through the power of Your message.

I know I am flawed. But please help me practice what I preach so that I can become an example for others to follow. May others look at my life and be drawn to You. Help me model a life of character and live in a virtuous and honorable way. May I draw others to You through my words, my conduct, and my life.

In Jesus' Name, Amen.

When I Need Approval

KEY SCRIPTURE:

And suddenly a voice came from heaven, saying,
"This is My beloved Son, in whom I am well pleased."
MATTHEW 3:17

Heavenly Father,

Remind me that You have chosen me and that I belong to You. Help me live like who I already am: an elect and beloved child of God.

Thank You for the reminder that I walk according to the blessing You have already provided. May I stand in the dignity and strong identity of being a child of the King, chosen before the foundation of the world.

I pray that Your Word would make me like a strong and graceful oak, established with roots reaching deep down into Your marvelous love. May I be the person You created me to be all the way to the core of my heart, abiding each day in Your unwavering acceptance.

In Jesus' Name I pray, Amen.

When I Have Lost My Joy

KEY SCRIPTURE:

*Restore to me the joy of your salvation, and
uphold me with a willing spirit.*
PSALM 51:12, ESV

Heavenly Father,

Sometimes I feel like my joy is lost; instead of being filled to overflowing, I feel empty. There are seasons of my life when I feel dry, even though You promised I have access to streams of living water. I choose to believe the promise of Your Word. I choose to believe that complete joy is found in You. Please help me tap into the eternal fountain of Your love.

Your Word says that joy is something You can restore, and I am asking for it now. I want to know the joy of the Lord as my strength and song. I want to rejoice in You no matter the circumstances I'm facing today. From the depths of my heart, I offer anthems of praise to You, my saving God. You are my God who never lets me go. You are my fountain of delight, ever-flowing with grace and peace. You, my Good Shepherd, lead me beside quiet waters and restore my soul. Thank You for the joy You give me.

In Jesus' Name, Amen.

When I'm in a Hard Season

KEY SCRIPTURE:

And you became followers of us and of the Lord, having received the word in much affliction, with joy of the Holy Spirit.
1 THESSALONIANS 1:6

Dear Father,

Teach me the mystery of receiving Your Word with joy even in the middle of affliction. I believe You are able to give that gift through the Holy Spirit. You can give me joy in trouble.

Bring forth true, genuine, heartfelt passion within me so that I can radiate joy in the midst of hardship. Help me worship with all my heart, confident about what You are doing in my life. For I know that when my faith is tested and I come through, I will experience joy that no other experience can compare to.

Let joy flood my soul because I have the reality of the Savior in my life. Though I've experienced a difficult time, may I declare that my God leads me to the other side. For You have been gracious to me.

In Jesus' Name, Amen.

When I Am Battling Hopelessness

KEY SCRIPTURE:

Why are you cast down, O my soul? And why are you disquieted within me? Hope in God; for I shall yet praise Him, the help of my countenance and my God.
PSALM 43:5

Father,

Thank You for Your Word that brings courage and Your Spirit, the Comforter. Help me fight the hopelessness that pulls me down like gravity to the bottom. I feel discouraged about what's gone wrong in my life, and I fear this despair may be permanent. But when my heart is discouraged within me, the consolation of Your Word buoys me with peace and joy.

Encourage me with Your presence, for I know You want me to have hope. Let my mouth be filled with praise because I remember how You saw me, saved me, and seated me with Christ when I was helpless and hopeless. May I not forget how good You have been to me. Let me remember Your guidance and blessing to me each day.

Allow true hope to spring from despair, for You have not forgotten me. Great is Your faithfulness, O God, my Heavenly Father.

In Jesus' Name, Amen.

PRAYER FOR...

When I Am
Victorious

KEY SCRIPTURE:

Since the children have flesh and blood, he too shared in their humanity so that by his death he might break the power of him who holds the power of death—that is, the devil—and free those who all their lives were held in slavery by their fear of death.
HEBREWS 2:14-15, NIV

Dear Lord Jesus,

You won the victory and broke the power of death. Thank You that the enemy is a defeated foe. Help me walk victoriously, not weighed down by the power of the enemy. Because of Your victory, I don't have to yield to the power of Satan.

The truth of the cross is that the enemy has no right to me, no power over me. One day the sentence against all evil will be carried out. But in the meantime, I am victorious in You.

You lead me to victory like a ship reaching the shore. After rough waters, I arrive safely at my destination, for You, Lord, are my captain of triumph.

In Your Name I pray, Amen.

PRAYER FOR...

When I Need a Heart for Others

KEY SCRIPTURE:

We give thanks to God always for you all, making mention of you in our prayers, remembering without ceasing your work of faith, labor of love, and patience of hope in our Lord Jesus Christ in the sight of our God and Father.
1 THESSALONIANS 1:2-3

God My Father,

I praise You for Your Word which encourages me. The believers in Thessalonica labored to the point of exhaustion out of love for their Savior. Help me also to see opportunities each day to express my faith in love. Preserve my heart from becoming calloused, cold, and indifferent.

For the sake of those who are lost in my community, help me keep that edge to my faith. May Your Spirit convict me whenever I seem content to sit on my hands; there is a work of faith and a labor of love yet to be fulfilled. Give me an energetic approach motivated by love in an outward way.

At the end of my life, I know I will not be able to say that I have done everything there is to do. But God, I want to look back and say that I did everything You asked me to do. Fill me with Your love for others.

In Jesus' Name, Amen.

When I Need to Surrender to God

KEY SCRIPTURE:

Be devoted to one another in love. Honor one another above yourselves. Never be lacking in zeal, but keep your spiritual fervor, serving the Lord. Be joyful in hope, patient in affliction, faithful in prayer.
ROMANS 12:10–12, NIV

Dear Father,

As I read Your Word and as I live for You each day, grow within my heart a burning desire to give everything to You. I declare today that You have everything of me there is to have.

I don't want to go through life, look back, and wish I had sold out fully to Jesus Christ. So I pray that You will impress upon me the importance of giving everything I have to You without reservation.

Help me to be committed to serving others and to reflecting You in all I do and say. Help me live an unbridled life in the will of God. And Father, keep me on schedule to see it done.

In Jesus' Name, Amen.

PRAYER FOR…

When I Feel
Afraid of Death

KEY SCRIPTURE:

Therefore they sought to take Him; but no one laid a hand on Him, because His hour had not yet come.
JOHN 7:30

Heavenly Father,

Thank You for this truth from Your glorious Word that Jesus' enemies could not lay a hand on Him because His hour had not yet come. In the same way that You protected and preserved the Savior, You are protecting and preserving me.

Help me to understand that I do not need to worry about death. Be the mighty fortress of my life, impenetrable and secure from all threats and harm.

Help me remember that as Your child, living in the center of Your will, I will live until You call me home to heaven.

May I live in the courage and confidence of this understanding that You are responsible for protecting me so that I might fulfill Your will in my life.

In Jesus' Name, Amen.

PRAYER FOR...

When It's
Hard to Forgive

KEY SCRIPTURE:

*And be kind to one another, tenderhearted, forgiving
one another, even as God in Christ forgave you.*
EPHESIANS 4:32

Dear Lord,

Thank You for Your great mercy. I was the one who put the crown of thorns on Your head, yet You offered me a crown in Your Kingdom—one without a thorn. I was the one who spat in Your face, yet You forgave me and died to save me. I was the one who thrust a spear into Your side, and still, You draw me close to Your heart.

How can I then harbor a resentful attitude toward another? May I release every grudge. May I forgive from my heart.

If You can forgive me, knowing who I am and all I've done to offend You, then surely I can forgive every person who wrongs me. Help me also to forgive when the other person does not even ask for forgiveness. This is how You've forgiven me.

Now it is my turn. Empower me by Your forgiving Spirit so that I can forgive like You.

In Jesus' Name, Amen.

When I Have a Big Decision to Make

KEY SCRIPTURE:

And let the peace of God rule in your hearts, to which
also you were called in one body; and be thankful.
COLOSSIANS 3:15

Dear Father,

You said that the peace You give is supposed to rule my heart, and I say "Yes" to that command. Let Your peace be the umpire of my heart. Have the final word, and make the ultimate call. I am comfortable with Your will and with Your plans because I know You always make the correct call.

Even so, I find myself needing to make more and more decisions as I move forward in this life. Often the best choice is not clear. In these moments, may I allow Your peace to rule and guide me.

I know that a decision is right when You give me real peace about it. When I don't have peace from You, help me change course. May I experience the reassurance of Your guidance and Your peace when I walk, when I lie down, when I rise up, when I sit, and when I stand.

In Jesus' Name, Amen.

PRAYER FOR...

When I Need God's Provision

KEY SCRIPTURE:

All creatures look to you to give them their food at the proper time. When you give it to them, they gather it up; when you open your hand, they are satisfied with good things.
PSALM 104:27–28, NIV

Dear Lord,

Thank You so much that whatever I need for this day is available from You. I can enter into Your presence and pray for that which I need. I come with my request; may it be purified by Your will.

Sometimes I worry about tomorrow's bread, but You've promised in Your Word to meet my needs. Let me be bold to come before You, asking for provision. I am an empty cup waiting to be filled, open for Your provision.

When I see all the ways You supply, may I remember that You are my ultimate source. Deliver me from worrying about the future when I know You tend to the sparrows, so why wouldn't You care for the crown of Your created work?

I give You the praise in the name of the Lord Jesus Christ, Amen.

PRAYER FOR...

When I Long for a Life Different From the World

KEY SCRIPTURE:

Therefore, I urge you, brothers and sisters, in view of God's
mercy, to offer your bodies as a living sacrifice, holy and
pleasing to God—this is your true and proper worship. Do not
conform to the pattern of this world, but be transformed by
the renewing of your mind. Then you will be able to test and
approve what God's will is—his good, pleasing and perfect will.
ROMANS 12:1-2, NIV

Heavenly Father,

It seems we spend more but have less, and we buy more but enjoy it less. There is an inner emptiness and bankruptcy in the world, and sometimes I feel it in my own soul. But, Lord, the only thing I know to counteract the deception of dissatisfaction is to get into Your Book and read what You have to say. When I do that, my mind is renewed, and my spirit begins to hope.

Let the searchlight of Your Word show me a better way. Help me glimpse Your great mercy and offer all I am in service to You. Wash me clean with the truth that it is possible to have the life I've always wanted—not the life I see on television or on social media but a life worth living—a life of worship and walking in Your good, pleasing, and perfect will. Thank You for blessing me with fulfillment and joy through Your Holy Spirit.

In Jesus' Name, Amen.

When I Feel Discouraged

KEY SCRIPTURE:

And David was greatly distressed; for the people spake
of stoning him, because the soul of all the people was
grieved, every man for his sons and for his daughters:
but David encouraged himself in the Lord his God.
1 SAMUEL 30:6, KJV

Dear Lord,

When I feel discouraged, help me not to just sit here and let hopelessness roll over me like a wave. Teach me how to encourage my heart in You. As I look through Your Word, help me remember Your greatness and the marvelous things You have done in my life. For You have not changed—You were the God of my hope in the past, and You are the God of my hope in the future.

You have lifted me from the ash heap and set my feet upon a rock. You hem me in, behind and before. You have given me authority to overcome all the power of the enemy.

Because of Your faithfulness, I choose to sing even though I feel like crying. Give me a song in the night, for Your light and truth guide me always.

In Jesus' Name, Amen.

PRAYER FOR...

When I
Feel Despair

KEY SCRIPTURE:

The Lord God is my strength; He will make my feet like deer's feet, and He will make me walk on my high hills.
HABAKKUK 3:19

Father,

I am confident my hope resides in You—the never-changing, ever-living, all-powerful God. I bless Your holy name today because of that truth. You are a God of hope. You demonstrate Your lovingkindess to me each day, and Your song is with me each night. You are the One who helps me to walk without stumbling on the difficult path before me. You strengthen me and uphold me. Although I may be walking through the valley of despair, I praise You that I don't have to live here. I can climb the heights to the great mountain peak and know Your joy and hope.

Please help me climb this mountain rather than sink into the valley of despair. I know it's going to be difficult. I know there will be sharp rocks and places where the path is unclear. But I also know You are with me and will always be with me. Please strengthen my feet so I can keep moving. Please strengthen my heart so I can keep believing. Please strengthen my mind so I can honor You and praise You even when the journey is difficult. Bring me to the top of the mountain, and may You be glorified today.

In Jesus' Name I pray, Amen.

When I Don't Know What to Pray

KEY SCRIPTURE:

Likewise the Spirit also helps in our weaknesses. For we do not know what we should pray for as we ought, but the Spirit Himself makes intercession for us with groanings which cannot be uttered.
ROMANS 8:26

Dear Lord,

There are moments when words fail me and I don't know what to pray. Now is one of those times. My heart is heavy, and my thoughts are confusing. But Your indwelling Spirit knows the inner turmoil of my life. I don't have to explain myself to Him because He knows me better than I know myself. He is the searcher of my heart.

Thank You that Your Spirit takes what I can't say today and lays it out in perfect form before You. He knows the burdens I'm carrying; He knows the worries and cares that are filling my mind. As He intercedes for me, bring peace where there is uncertainty and clarity where there is confusion.

Lord Jesus, help me remember the greatness of my God and rest in the knowledge that You hear my prayers. I give You all the praise.

In Your Name, Amen.

PRAYER FOR...

When I Carry Regret for My Past

KEY SCRIPTURE:

For as the heavens are high above the earth, so great is His mercy toward those who fear Him; as far as the east is from the west, so far has He removed our transgressions from us.
PSALM 103:11-12

Dear Lord,

At times I allow the past and its failures and mistakes to terrorize me, and yet the God I serve is the one true constant in all the world. You are always the same. You are merciful. And I can come to You with absolute confidence that You have forgiven me.

Nothing disqualifies me from Your forgiveness in the present and Your forgiveness in the days to come. You are here now to meet me; my past cannot keep me from You. For You are the everlasting God, and I am talking to You in prayer. You have told me in Your Word that You will forgive my sins and that You redeem my life.

I'm asking today that you would take my past, present, and future and lead me in the path of peace. Forgive me for what I have done in the past, and remind me that Your mercy and forgiveness are great.

In Jesus' Name, Amen.

When I
Need a Friend

KEY SCRIPTURE:

As iron sharpens iron, so a man sharpens
the countenance of his friend.
PROVERBS 27:17

Father,

A good friend is a gift. And I'm asking for that gift now. I pray for a friend I can meet with and together deal with the tough issues of life. Give me a friendship in which we can learn from one another, share our viewpoints, and be truly understood.

May I have a friendship in which we share the most important things in our lives. Father, may I grow the kind of friendship where we are both sharpened and strengthened by one another. Help us share what You are doing in our lives, improve one another, and take advantage of opportunities to deal with the issues in our lives face to face.

Teach me to be the kind of friend who offers this to another, someone who can be trusted and counted on. Teach me to be a friend to others like You are to me.

Thank You, in Jesus' Name, Amen.

When I Need to Choose Obedience

KEY SCRIPTURE:

Choose for yourselves this day whom you will serve....
But as for me and my house, we will serve the Lord.
JOSHUA 24:15

Lord,

I pray that You will help me read Your Word with a view to doing it. Thank You for Joshua's example of prioritizing obedience to Your words. And may this be my motto: I will read Your Book to do it. I will study Your Word to obey it.

Send me out into this day, Lord, with the great potential of obedience. May that obedience be the key to my joy as I walk each day in faithfulness to Your Word.

Please give me some difficult things to do, and please let me not be satisfied with easy obedience. Give me some hard obedience—obedience that exacts from me a greater measure of faith and commitment than I have known in the past.

I pray that You will forgive me for being disobedient to You. There have been so many times I knew what to do but did not do it. Please forgive me for that. Help me to strike out in a new direction of open obedience to You in all that I say and do.

In Jesus' Name, Amen.

When I Want to Demonstrate Kindness

KEY SCRIPTURE:

Grace and peace be multiplied to you in the knowledge of God and of Jesus our Lord, as His divine power has given to us all things that pertain to life and godliness, through the knowledge of Him who called us by glory and virtue, by which have been given to us exceedingly great and precious promises, that through these you may be partakers of the divine nature, having escaped the corruption that is in the world through lust.
2 PETER 1:2-4

Heavenly Father,

Teach me to live in pursuit of life and godliness. You have given me Your power and Your provision; help me download this into my life. Lord, Your promises are great and exceedingly precious. When I have these, Your Word says that I have everything I need for life and godliness—not some things, not most things, not many things—but everything! Help me remember that You have given me the power for godliness, the power to live in ways that are godly.

When You show my spirit a way of offering radical kindness, may I not wait until tomorrow. Help me do it immediately. I want to offer kindness to my brother, my neighbor, and my family, just like You offered radical kindness and love to me—even when I didn't deserve it. Thank You for Your kindness.

In Jesus' Name, Amen.

When the Future Is Uncertain

KEY SCRIPTURE:

*As you do not know what is the way of the wind, or how the
bones grow in the womb of her who is with child, so you
do not know the works of God who makes everything.*
ECCLESIASTES 11:5

Father,

Thank You for this portion of Your Word that teaches me to trust through the unknown. I don't know where the wind will blow, but I am diligent in Your work each day. I pray that You will help me be committed in my spirit to walk boldly with You in this time.

As uncertain as it may be, I'm going to embrace it. As discouraging as it can be, I'm going to enjoy it. Father, help me learn, move forward, and be strong through Your grace.

I also pray that You will continue to use me to make a difference in the world. When I feel tempted to hold back instead of getting involved, guide me to see the importance of the part I play. I believe that even when darkness falls, Your light is certain to overcome it.

In Jesus' Name, Amen.

PRAYER FOR...

When I'm Starting My Day

KEY SCRIPTURE:

This is the day the Lord has made; we
will rejoice and be glad in it.
PSALM 118:24

Heavenly Father,

Thank You for the power of Your Word to lead me on the path of righteousness. These words remind me to praise You because You have given me this day.

Guide me to enjoy every day with everything I have. Thank You, Lord, for this new day. Thank You for the privilege of waking up in this community. Thank You for the light I see and the air I breathe.

Though I cannot predict the twists and turns of each day, help me to look out into the world in which I live and say, "Thank You, Father, for today's opportunities." Through Your Holy Spirit, I choose to be fully engaged with life.

In Jesus' Name, Amen.

When I Am Confused

KEY SCRIPTURE:

*And moreover, because the Preacher was wise, he
still taught the people knowledge; yes, he pondered
and sought out and set in order many proverbs.*
ECCLESIASTES 12:9

Heavenly Father,

You were the source of Solomon's wisdom when he reigned as king and when he wrote his many proverbs. You spoke through him to provide good counsel to Your people, and You continue to speak through Your Word to provide wisdom to all who follow You, including me.

I need Your wisdom today because I am feeling confused. I don't know what to do or where to turn. I feel the lack of wisdom in my own mind and heart, and the knowledge of my weakness makes me feel afraid. So please be close to me.

Please speak to me through Your Word today. Give me wisdom, clarity, and discernment so that I can honor You with my words and my actions. I'm so grateful that I can rely on You.

In Jesus' Name I pray, Amen.

When I Need to Trust and Obey

KEY SCRIPTURE:

Trust in the Lord with all your heart, and lean not on your own understanding; in all your ways acknowledge Him, and He shall direct your paths.... Fear the Lord and depart from evil. It will be health to your flesh, and strength to your bones.
PROVERBS 3:5-8

Dear Father,

I praise You for the truth and freedom found in Your Word. I know that a life filled with joy, happiness, and meaning comes from fearing You and following Your commands.

There is just no way to beat that formula. Help me heed Your Word, to trust You and not to rely on my own wisdom, to remember that You will direct my way.

Help me look to You in absolute awe, utter respect, and majesty. Guide my spirit to lift You up, never take Your name in vain, or do anything that would tarnish Your reputation. For I know that the best way to enjoy life is to fear You and keep Your commandments.

In Jesus' Name I pray, Amen.

PRAYER FOR...

When I Feel
Unloved

KEY SCRIPTURE:

Now before the Feast of the Passover, when Jesus knew that His hour had come that He should depart from this world to the Father, having loved His own who were in the world, He loved them to the end.
JOHN 13:1

Dearest Lord Jesus,

Thank You for Your selfless love. You teach me the meaning of Your *agape* love—loving someone even if You never receive anything back. I praise You, Lord, for Your incredibly patient love, always nudging me toward maturity.

You don't just love me when I am attending church or doing good works; You love me no matter what. Your love encompasses my lifelong journey. Your love is the constant thread that runs through my story from beginning to end.

When I don't know what to do, help me know that the best answer is love, for Your love helps me know how to act in every situation. Your *agape* love is the key to my heart and my life. I praise You because Your love gives me the courage to serve You.

In Your Name, Amen.

When I Am Overwhelmed

KEY SCRIPTURE:

And we have known and believed the love that
God has for us. God is love, and he who abides
in love abides in God, and God in him.
1 JOHN 4:16

Heavenly Father,

You know everything that is pressing down on me right now. You know the demands that are placed on my time. You know the strain I feel financially. You know where I am struggling in key relationships. You know more about my physical and emotional health than I ever will. You know all about me, so please help me!

Right now what I am being asked to give feels like more than I possess. I feel insufficient for the demands of life. Because of the things that have happened to me and the pressure I face, I find myself feeling a sense of total inadequacy for what I need to do. Help me lean on the love of Christ.

I declare right now that my heart is completely open to You. Please help me with this problem. I know You love me. I accept Your love. Help me grow in the love You have for me. May I be able to relax in the face of difficulty because You are at work through my words and hands. Help me sense Your loving presence with me.

In Jesus' Name, Amen.

When I'm Preparing to Serve in Church

KEY SCRIPTURE:

Jesus, knowing that the Father had given all things into His hands, and that He had come from God and was going to God, rose from supper and laid aside His garments, took a towel and girded Himself. After that, He poured water into a basin and began to wash the disciples' feet, and to wipe them with the towel with which He was girded.
JOHN 13:3-5

Dear Savior,

Your loving service amazes me. I read about the flustered disciples feeling Your hand cleaning their feet, wiping away the mud. You, whose sandals they were not worthy to untie—You washed their feet. You served because of Your love.

I know that love is the way I get through life. I know that when I truly know Your love, I will want to serve other people. Let Your love resonate within me, and may I be so overwhelmed by it that I want to share it with others and to serve in inexplicable ways because this quality of divine love courses through my spiritual veins.

May Your love motivate me so that I recognize and heed the call to serve when it comes.

In Jesus' Name, Amen.

PRAYER FOR...

When I Doubt
God's Love

KEY SCRIPTURE:

We love because he first loved us.
1 JOHN 4:19, NIV

Heavenly Father,

I want to proclaim this truth from the mountaintops: You love me! I give You praise today because You loved me first—before I was even aware of You. Your love is the foundation for who I am, and it is the basis for everything I hope to do.

Help me remember that love always comes from You. And that because You love me, I have both the privilege and the responsibility to love others.

It's painful when I don't feel loved by other people, especially when I don't feel loved by those I care about most. There are times when I'm afraid of being rejected or when I'm afraid of feeling unloved. Please remind me of the awareness of Your love for me.

Please ground me once again in the reality of Your love for me. And help me live confidently from that solid foundation.

In Jesus' Name, Amen.

PRAYER FOR…

When I'm Experiencing Stress at Work

KEY SCRIPTURE:

*And whatever you do, do it heartily, as to the Lord and not
to men, knowing that from the Lord you will receive the
reward of the inheritance; for you serve the Lord Christ.*
COLOSSIANS 3:23-24

Dear Lord,

Your Holy Word guides me at every moment, including as I go about my work. I want to be Your servant even as I work and serve those in authority over me. Keep me from allowing the conditions of my environment to affect how I go about my tasks.

As an employee, help me devote my full attention to each job and each task with singleness of heart and skillfulness of hand. When I'm weary in the work, remind me that Your Holy Spirit gives me all of the power and motivation I need.

I am stating my desire in prayer to serve You at every opportunity. Even the little mundane tasks that I don't enjoy—each one is an opportunity to conform myself to Your will and Your work.

Whatever I put my hand to, help me do it with all my might.

In Jesus' Name, Amen.

PRAYER FOR...

When I Have Challenges With My Boss

KEY SCRIPTURE:

*Servants, be submissive to your masters with all
fear, not only to the good and gentle, but also
to the harsh. For this is commendable.*
1 PETER 2:18-19

Father,

Thank You for the instruction and correction in Your Word.
You tell me I do not get off the hook just because my boss may be
harsh at times. Lord, I believe You have placed me here to show the
difference it makes to have Christ in my heart and the Holy Spirit in
control of my life.

Help me be the employee You made me to be, working with
all my heart. And let my hard work be part of my testimony as
a Christian.

Let those in authority observe me working with a sincere heart,
not just showing up to punch a clock but showing integrity and
excellence in my tasks. I pray that my respect for You will surface in
honorable interactions with those I work for as a testimony to them.

I know I am working unto the Lord, not for human masters, since
You have promised me an inheritance. May Your favor rest upon me
and establish the work of my hands.

In Jesus' Name, Amen.

PRAYER FOR...

When I Feel
Insignificant

KEY SCRIPTURE:

I will praise You, for I am fearfully and wonderfully made; marvelous are Your works, and that my soul knows very well. My frame was not hidden from You, when I was made in secret, and skillfully wrought in the lowest parts of the earth. Your eyes saw my substance, being yet unformed. And in Your book they all were written, the days fashioned for me, when as yet there were none of them.
PSALM 139:14-16

Dear Lord,

I praise You for creating me. You knew me and loved me before I was even born. In this fallen world I can lose sight of who I am. Help me remember my identity as someone who is "fearfully and wonderfully made."

Help me live for You, take responsibility for my relationships, and steward the resources You've given me. Then Lord, help me make a difference in this world.

You know what each of my days will hold; equip me to use them wisely for Your glory. I love You and want to serve You with all of my heart.

In Jesus' Name, Amen.

When I Doubt God's Purpose for Me

KEY SCRIPTURE:

He chose us in Him before the foundation of the world, that we should be holy and without blame before Him in love, having predestined us to adoption as sons by Jesus Christ to Himself, according to the good pleasure of His will, to the praise of the glory of His grace, by which He made us accepted in the Beloved.
EPHESIANS 1:4-6

Dear Father,

You chose me to be Your child before the foundation of the world. Even then you knew everything about me and what I would become; even then You had a purpose for me. Lord, no creature in all of creation enjoys an intimate, personal relationship with the God of heaven, yet You give me the rights and privileges of Your child. Your Word teaches that the meaning of man starts and ends with the glory of God. Help me truly meditate on this reality.

Help me not to live just for the moment but also to find deep and lasting meaning in You. Through Jesus Christ living in me, may I have a new understanding, a new sense of purpose and meaning. Because of You, I can recover confidence in who I am and why I am here. I thank You for it.

In Jesus' Name, Amen.

When I Don't Want to Do What God Is Asking

KEY SCRIPTURE:

Let this mind be in you which was also in Christ Jesus, who, being in the form of God, did not consider it robbery to be equal with God, but made Himself of no reputation, taking the form of a bondservant, and coming in the likeness of men. And being found in appearance as a man, He humbled Himself and became obedient to the point of death, even the death of the cross.
PHILIPPIANS 2:5-8

Lord Jesus,

I know from Scripture that You did not want to endure the cross. You asked the Father if there was another way for You to achieve Your mission of salvation. And when the answer was given, You submitted Yourself to the Father's will. I am choosing to follow Your example today. Please help me.

I pray that You will help me to open my heart to you and say, "I've tried it my own way. I realize now what's wrong. Give me the grace to choose Your way."

Help me to see the meaning infused in each hour, each day, living with a sense of adventure in the plan You have for me. Help me accept Your will and Your plan even when I don't like it or understand it.

In Your Name, Amen.

When the World Feels Out of Control

KEY SCRIPTURE:

The Lord has established His throne in heaven, and His kingdom rules over all.
PSALM 103:19

Lord God,

I believe that You are in charge. You are on the throne, and You always will be. Whenever mankind has tried to prove he's in control, he has been frustrated and thwarted. Again and again, You have said that You are the Lord and You rule in the heavens and in the earth and in the hearts of men.

Instead of letting anxiety rule and uncertainty prevail, I declare today that You rule and reign in all things—from sea to sea and from time to eternity. There is no truth in all the world that comforts me more than this: My God is in control. I believe that nothing is happening that hasn't passed through Your fingers and will ultimately be sanctified by You.

You are the Sovereign God. When I see what's happening across this world, I choose to turn off the television, stop scrolling the Internet, open my Bible, bow my head, and say, "I know the One who's in charge."

In Jesus' Name, Amen.

When I've Been Wronged

KEY SCRIPTURE:

But as for you, you meant evil against me; but
God meant it for good, in order to bring it about
as it is this day, to save many people alive.
GENESIS 50:20

Heavenly Father,

I praise You for Your sovereignty—You are in control. Somehow the prison that Joseph thought would end his life led him into Your purposes. Somehow the stormy Red Sea which Pharaoh thought had trapped his enemies in Exodus became the avenue of their deliverance. But it wasn't "somehow"; it was sovereignty. The God of heaven was showing who was in control.

In every test help me declare, like Joseph: "They tried to hurt me. They tried to destroy me. They tried to kill me. But God was in charge, and God brought me through."

No matter what evil comes against me, I trust that You will use it for good to bring about Your purpose. When I don't understand why things are happening, help me step back and realize I'm down on the floor and You're in the captain's seat. And I trust You, knowing that You're moving me to the place where You want me to be.

In Jesus' Name, Amen.

When I Need Help Taming My Tongue

KEY SCRIPTURE:

Let no corrupt communication proceed out of your
mouth, but that which is good to the use of edifying,
that it may minister grace unto the hearers.
EPHESIANS 4:29, KJV

Dear Father,

Thank You for the relationships in my life. Help me value them by being open and trustworthy in my communication. I want to be the kind of person who always speaks positively and encouragingly, but I know I have the capacity to harm others with my words.

I confess that my speech often becomes corrupted by words, attitudes, and topics that are not honoring to You. Please forgive me. Please help me edify and impart grace, strengthening those close to me. Help me build them up and not tear them down.

Help me encourage and minister grace to those You bring into my life. I pray in all my relationships that I may work diligently to take care of what You've given me.

In Jesus' Name I pray, Amen.

PRAYER FOR...

When I Don't
Feel Like Praying

KEY SCRIPTURE:

Let us therefore come boldly to the throne of grace, that we
may obtain mercy and find grace to help in time of need.
HEBREWS 4:16

Dear Father,

Sometimes I do not pray as I ought, but Your Word tells me that it is my priority. You tell me to come boldly before Your throne, and You promise to give me mercy and grace in my time of need. And now help me to bring my requests and my cares to You and to pour out my heart to You as Jesus did.

Remove the barriers that are keeping me from talking to You through prayer. May my heart be still before You and the cares of the day not fill my mind.

Draw the veil aside, Father, and allow me to walk into the holy of holies with my High Priest. Let me approach the secret place of the tabernacle of the Most High and join Jesus, my Intercessor, in prayer.

In Jesus' Name, Amen.

When Life
Feels Unjust

KEY SCRIPTURE:

I know that the Lord will maintain the cause of the afflicted,
and justice for the poor. Surely the righteous shall give thanks
to Your name; the upright shall dwell in Your presence.
PSALM 140:12-13

Heavenly Father,

Where are You when I need You? You don't seem to do anything about injustice in the world and in my community. You don't do anything about injustice in the country. You don't do anything about the injustice in my life. It seems like You are fleeing from me. I don't know where You are. But I know that You know where I am.

I thank You for the honesty of the psalmists. Thank You for the examples of openness with You and the encouragement to bring my questions to You. Touch my heart and fill me with strength and confidence that You, the one true God, know me and hear me.

You are just and right. I may not see Your justice enacted here on earth, but I am confident that You will perfectly judge unrighteousness in Your timing.

In Jesus' Name, Amen.

When I'm Pleading With God

KEY SCRIPTURE:

Concerning this thing I pleaded with the Lord three times that it might depart from me. And He said to me, "My grace is sufficient for you, for My strength is made perfect in weakness." Therefore most gladly I will rather boast in my infirmities, that the power of Christ may rest upon me.
2 CORINTHIANS 12:8-9

Heavenly Father,

I feel like echoing Paul's sentiments right now: Please get this thing out of my life! Please provide some relief! I don't know if You will grant my request, but I'm grateful to know I'm not the only one who faces obstacles that I wish would go away. Thank You for the example of Your servant Paul.

Even though I feel like I can't go on like this, help me accept that You may be giving me the same answer you gave Paul. If You do not remove this hindrance in my life, I know You will help me get through it. Reassure my spirit with Your Word right now: Your grace is sufficient for me, and Your strength comes into its own in my weakness. Give me the grace to see this difficulty as a gift that pushes me to my knees and leads me to the only place where I find help in my time of need.

In Jesus' Name, Amen.

When I Am Feeling Weak

KEY SCRIPTURE:

*Therefore I take pleasure in infirmities, in reproaches,
in needs, in persecutions, in distresses, for Christ's
sake. For when I am weak, then I am strong.*
2 CORINTHIANS 12:10

Heavenly Father,

The Bible describes Your Kingdom as a collection of paradoxes. The key to being first is to be last. The key to being the greatest is to make myself least. You resist the proud and lift up the humble. You have declared that the foolish are wise and the wise are foolish. And You have affirmed that when I feel weak is actually the moment when I am strong.

Please confirm that truth in my life right now because I feel weak. Please remind me through Your Spirit that You are up to something great. Help me to have a new attitude of rejoicing amid ailments, difficulty, need, persecution, and distress. You are my God, and You are the greatest wealth I could ever have. Even full health and the prosperity of the world could never compare to the gift of Your Spirit, the encouragement of Your friendship, and the comfort of Your presence. Thank You that You deliver me from all my troubles.

In Jesus' Name, Amen.

When I'm Thinking About Giving Up

KEY SCRIPTURE:

My foot has held fast to His steps; I have kept His way and not turned aside. I have not departed from the commandment of His lips; I have treasured the words of His mouth more than my necessary food.
JOB 23:11-12

Lord,

I don't know what You're up to, but I'm in the furnace, and the only thing that's keeping me are the words that I've received from You. If I didn't have these words, I wouldn't be able to make it.

Please encourage me through Your Word today. Help me hold fast to Your steps and stay true to Your way. May I treasure Your commands like a gem I hold close to my heart. And keep me from fearing the fire, for the furnace can only make gold purer and brighter. In pain and anguish, when it's blazing and hot, help me hear Your voice.

Confirm in my spirit that You are with me, that You are close to me in the midst of this trial, and that You are calling me to stand firm. May it be obvious on the other side of this valley that You used these circumstances to make me more like Christ.

In Jesus' Name I pray, Amen.

When I'm in Awe of God

KEY SCRIPTURE:

In this manner, therefore, pray: Our Father
in heaven, hallowed be Your name.
MATTHEW 6:9

Dear Father,

You are in heaven. When I stop to think of this reality, I remember that the earth is Your footstool and You are the God of majesty and might. You are the glorious King, and You are worthy of all my worship.

You are surrounded by the angelic host. You sit on the throne of majesty, and You are ministered to by all the creatures of glory.

Lord God, I think of all the regality I can imagine, distilled from all the kingdoms of this world, multiply it a hundred times a hundred, and I haven't even touched the surface of the glory and majesty of my Father who is in heaven. May I always stand in awe of who You are.

In Christ's Name I pray, Amen.

When I Feel Inadequate

KEY SCRIPTURE:

For we are His workmanship, created in Christ
Jesus for good works, which God prepared
beforehand that we should walk in them.
EPHESIANS 2:10

Dear Father,

I affirm the truth of this passage that I am Your workmanship. I was created by You through the spoken command of Jesus, my Savior. I was created as part of Your plan. And I was created with a purpose—created to accomplish good works that You prepared for me to accomplish from the beginning of time.

Thank You for the gifts You've given me. I know I won't get where You want me to go with my gifts alone; my abilities cannot bring about all that You have planned. So thank You for these gifts. Use them as You want to. I depend on You and You alone.

I declare today that You are enough, that You are sufficient. Fill me with Your power. I dedicate myself to Your service. I want You to lead me; I want You to guide me. Help me to walk in the good works that You have prepared for me.

In Jesus' Name, Amen.

PRAYER FOR...

When I Feel Incapable

KEY SCRIPTURE:

*Not that we are sufficient of ourselves to think of anything
as being from ourselves, but our sufficiency is from God.*
2 CORINTHIANS 3:5

Heavenly Father,

I'm grateful that You want to use me and that You have a plan for my life. I know I'm not too weak for You to use, but help me not to be too strong for You to use either. Help me not to be so full of my problems or pride that there's no room for You.

Take the emptiness I feel and fill it with Yourself. And when I don't measure up to the world's standards of appearance or sophistication, may I find peace and confidence in You. I renounce my dependence upon my abilities or others' approval and put my dependence upon You.

Help me think of myself with sober judgment by the faith You have given me, for I am a servant of Almighty God. And if You, my God, had not done something in my life, I would have lost my way. Thank You for the all-sufficient transformation of the Gospel and Your almighty power.

In Jesus' Name, Amen.

PRAYER FOR...

When I Forget
Who I Am

KEY SCRIPTURE:

But when the fullness of the time had come, God sent forth
His Son, born of a woman, born under the law, to redeem
those who were under the law, that we might receive the
adoption as sons. And because you are sons, God has
sent forth the Spirit of His Son into your hearts, crying
out, "Abba, Father!" Therefore you are no longer a slave but
a son, and if a son, then an heir of God through Christ.
GALATIANS 4:4-7

Dear Heavenly Father,

Thank You for the incredible gift of the new birth. Thank You for creating a way for us, who were estranged and far from You, to come into fellowship with You so that we can call You Father.

What an incredible thing it is to imagine looking up into the face of a loving Heavenly Father who cares for me. Help me wrap my arms around the truth that You are personal and You are pleased with me. I am not a slave; I am Your beloved child. Give me a whole new understanding of the Fatherhood of God. Teach me through Your Spirit within me so that I can address You as "Abba, Father!"

Thank You that You have set Your affection on me, and You know what things I need before I ask. I praise You that I can walk right into Your presence, Almighty God who always hears and embraces me.

In Jesus' Name, Amen.

When I Want to Thank God for My Affliction

KEY SCRIPTURE:

Therefore we do not lose heart. Even though our outward man is perishing, yet the inward man is being renewed day by day. For our light affliction, which is but for a moment, is working for us a far more exceeding and eternal weight of glory.... For the things which are seen are temporary, but the things which are not seen are eternal.
2 CORINTHIANS 4:16-18

My God,

I have never thanked You for the pain of my life. I have thanked You a thousand times for my blessings, but I rarely thank You for my affliction. Lord, I look forward to a future when I will be free of this burden, receiving glory as compensation for the cross I have borne in this life. But I have never once imagined my cross as glory now. Teach me the present glory of my cross.

Teach me the value of the work You are doing in my life. Show me that the affliction of today is temporary. Show me what matters for eternity.

In Jesus' Name, Amen.

When I Need to Experience God's Power

KEY SCRIPTURE:

That you may walk worthy of the Lord, fully pleasing Him, being fruitful in every good work and increasing in the knowledge of God; strengthened with all might, according to His glorious power, for all patience and longsuffering with joy; giving thanks to the Father.
COLOSSIANS 1:10-12

Lord Jesus,

I praise You for Your Word and for Your provision of power. Help me come to the end of everything in myself and all I rely upon. May I recognize that my weakness is the very conduit of your blessing and power. I know You will give me the grace I need to get through this. Thank You for giving me the strength to be Your ambassador.

May my weakness serve to magnify Your greatness and Your glory in such a way that no one will ever be able to explain my life in human terms. In my weakness, allow me to be a channel of Your great power.

Let it become no longer about me but all about Christ. Allow this weakness to help me put aside any gift or ability I have so that the power of Almighty God fills the vacuum.

In Jesus' Name I pray, Amen.

When I Forget Who God Is

KEY SCRIPTURE:

He said to them, "When you pray, say: Our Father
in heaven, hallowed be Your name. Your kingdom
come. Your will be done on earth as it is in heaven."
LUKE 11:2

Dear Lord,

I ask You to forgive me when I forget to acknowledge who You are and worship You as You deserve. I thank You and praise You for all that the Word of God reveals You to be. When I think about being a sinner, I remember that You are Jehovah Tsidkenu, the Lord my righteousness. When I think about my need to be holy, I think of Jehovah M'Kaddesh, the Lord who sanctifies me. And when I feel anxious, I worship Jehovah Shalom, the Lord who is my peace. There are times when I feel lonely and I need Jehovah Shammah because You are the Lord who is there.

When I'm sick, I look to Jehovah Rapha—the Lord who heals me. When I have financial needs, You are Jehovah Jireh, the Lord who will provide. When I lack self-esteem, help me remember that You are my banner, Jehovah Nissi, proudly claiming me as Your own. When my life and my direction are unclear, I need Jehovah Rohi, the Lord who shepherds me. As I remember and revere Your name, thank You that I come to know the Person behind the name. Let Your greatness be impressed upon my spirit.

I praise and thank You in the name of Jesus, Amen.

PRAYER FOR...

When I Long to Worship

KEY SCRIPTURE:

Let the words of my mouth and the meditation of my heart be acceptable in Your sight, O Lord, my strength and my Redeemer.
PSALM 19:14

Heavenly Father,

Thank You for the Word of God that teaches me to respect and revere You. You are worthy of my praise and deserving of my trust. May the whole of my life be a source of delight to You, bringing honor to the name which I bear. Your Word teaches that You seek those who will worship You in spirit and truth.

Lord, show me that You love to be worshiped and praised and that You call me to lift up Your name. You know the requests I have—I need daily bread and protection and wisdom.

But before I come with requests, may I come first with reverence to worship You and acknowledge who You are. You are great and mighty, worthy of all praise. And with great love in my heart, I say that I love You and thank You.

In Jesus' Name, Amen.

PRAYER FOR...

When I Want to Form a Habit of Prayer

KEY SCRIPTURE:

Now in the morning, having risen a long while
before daylight, He went out and departed to
a solitary place; and there He prayed.
MARK 1:35

Lord Jesus,

I sense the power and impact of Your prayer life—getting up well before dawn to be alone and pray to the Father. I know that prayer is only learned through practice, so help me make it a habit. I'm here before You today, and I want Your will in my life. I know that more important than anything else is that I am right with You. For if I'm wrong with You, everything else is wrong.

Help me continue to see the vital importance of my relationship with You. I don't want to neglect that. And in light of all of the other pressures in my life, help me to see that it takes discipline to be godly and that I must involve myself in a routine, daily partnering with Your Spirit to see the spiritual ground of my heart cultivated. Help me always remember to prioritize my relationship with You. Give me the power and insight to pray more effectively and never lose my fervor and desire.

In Your Name, Amen.

When I Need Protection

KEY SCRIPTURE:

And do not lead us into temptation,
but deliver us from the evil one.
MATTHEW 6:13

Heavenly Father,

Today I pray that You will protect me from evil, and keep me out of the way of temptation. The evil one's ever around, seeking whom he may devour.

Deliver me. I need Your help. Protect me. Put a hedge around me and those close to me. Keep me. You promise to be faithful and not to allow me to be tempted beyond what I am able to handle and to make a way of escape for me.

Help me to see the way of escape that You provide for me. I revel in the truth that You know how to deliver the godly out of trial. So I pray this prayer to You, God.

Protect me and my loved ones. You will keep in perfect peace the one who trusts in You.

In Jesus' Name, Amen.

When I Have Failed

KEY SCRIPTURE:

We are hard-pressed on every side, yet not crushed; we are perplexed, but not in despair; persecuted, but not forsaken; struck down, but not destroyed—always carrying about in the body the dying of the Lord Jesus, that the life of Jesus also may be manifested in our body. For we who live are always delivered to death for Jesus' sake, that the life of Jesus also may be manifested in our mortal flesh.
2 CORINTHIANS 4:8-11

Father,

Thank You that I can look to the Scripture for help when I am under pressure and when I fail. Your Word teaches that I will fail because I am human. There are times when I don't want to accept that reality, but I'm grateful that You are not surprised by my failure. You know who I am and that I don't have it all together. When I experience defeat, You know I am a vessel of clay. You know I will stumble in many things, yet You call me into Your purpose again and again.

For all the times that I have failed through sin, forgive me. Thank You for not dealing with me according to my sin or treating me as I deserve. You give me a fresh start, even after monumental failure. Just as Your resurrection power shone through Jesus' death, Your life and glory will manifest in and through me. Let my mistakes and failures be a window that lets the light of Jesus shine in.

In Jesus' Name, Amen.

When I Need to Stop Judging Others

KEY SCRIPTURE:

The Pharisee stood and prayed thus with himself, "God, I thank You that I am not like other men—extortioners, unjust, adulterers, or even as this tax collector. I fast twice a week; I give tithes of all that I possess." And the tax collector, standing afar off, would not so much as raise his eyes to heaven, but beat his breast, saying, "God, be merciful to me a sinner!" I tell you, this man went down to his house justified rather than the other; for everyone who exalts himself will be humbled, and he who humbles himself will be exalted.
LUKE 18:11-14

Dear Father,

Thank You that You do not judge based on appearances—You search a person's heart. Examine mine right now. I confess that I am tempted to evaluate things through my own human eyes, judging whether someone is a success or a failure based on appearances. Lord, help me be careful because You and You alone can see the reality of someone's heart.

Give me grace to pay closer attention to my own heart and the life You have given me, to take the speck out of my own eye first. I thank You that the ground at the foot of the cross is level. I kneel before You today, asking You to be merciful to me, a sinner. Instead of being right in my own eyes, make me right with You.

In Jesus' Name, Amen.

When I'm Facing Unexpected Circumstances

KEY SCRIPTURE:

My brethren, count it all joy when you fall into various trials, knowing that the testing of your faith produces patience. But let patience have its perfect work, that you may be perfect and complete, lacking nothing.
JAMES 1:2-4

Heavenly Father,

Thank You that Your Word teaches that I can be filled with joy even in the midst of difficult situations. I know that this joy is found in understanding, committing, and submitting to the truths of Your Word. I'm not asking for happiness that depends on circumstances; I'm asking for joy that depends on Jesus. When the unexpected occurs, help me to find joy in the journey. I'm coming to the source of joy, for You said that when I ask, I will receive the fullness of joy and live out joy in my relationships with others.

Let Your Word so affect my life that the circumstance is not the controlling influence but rather the principles of Your Word to which I've submitted my attitude. Above and beyond it all, give me a deep, abounding joy that the world cannot dilute or destroy.

In Jesus' Name, Amen.

When I Need to Read Scripture

KEY SCRIPTURE:

You will show me the path of life; in Your presence is fullness of joy; at Your right hand are pleasures forevermore.
PSALM 16:11

Dear God,

Help me not to want a shortcut but to submit daily to Your truth. Give me the strength and resolve to pick up Your Word even when I don't feel like it—when it seems like a war is going on in my own heart.

In obedience to You may I study Your Book and discipline my mind to understand its truths. For I know something will happen in the process and suddenly the feeling that I couldn't conjure up in advance—that feeling of joy and excitement about God—will return.

Let the floodgates open as I abide in Your love, Father. And may the joy of Your salvation fill my soul. I praise You and thank You for it.

In Christ's Name, Amen.

When I Need to Submit to the Holy Spirit

KEY SCRIPTURE:

The kingdom of God is not eating and drinking, but righteousness and peace and joy in the Holy Spirit.
ROMANS 14:17

Heavenly Father,

Thank You for Your indwelling Spirit and the gifts of Your Kingdom. I know that joy and peace are outward expressions of the inward control of the Holy Spirit in my life. May I submit the inward authority of my very being to You. And as You take control, may I become more like Christ.

I recognize that when I am not controlled by the Spirit of God, I lose joy in my personal experience. Help me close the gap between my desire to control my own life and my desire to submit to the control of the Spirit of God.

When that gap closes, I know I will discover more and more of the joy of the Lord permeating my life, bubbling over like a brook into the lives of others.

In Jesus' Name, Amen.

When I Need Joy

KEY SCRIPTURE:

These things I have spoken to you, that My joy may
remain in you, and that your joy may be full.
JOHN 15:11

Lord Jesus,

Thank You that I don't have to manufacture a feeling of happiness because You give me Your everlasting joy. Please give me a transfusion of joy right from Your heart into my spiritual being. I know that Yours is the only joy that takes me through difficulty and hard times. May I not be satisfied with the counterfeit happiness found in other places.

I ask that Your joy would not be fleeting. May it remain in me, and may it be full. Protect me against circumstances and other people who seek to rob me of the joy You provide. Let Your inexpressible and glorious joy be mine, becoming part of my lifestyle each day. Let it overflow into every interaction and relationship. Let it be a perpetual joy that goes with me in every experience. May Your joy in me be my daily strength.

In Jesus' Name, Amen.

PRAYER FOR...

When I
Want to Grow
in Hospitality

KEY SCRIPTURE:

Be hospitable to one another without grumbling.
1 PETER 4:9

Father,

I pray that You will develop within me a spirit of openness to friends and neighbors. Give me a spirit of willingness to risk involvement and generosity, even if it costs me.

Help me show mercy and hospitality to every person You put in my path. Against the backdrop of this closed-hearted age, help me shine forth as a wonderful light in this world.

May I constantly be on the lookout for someone to whom I can minister using the gift of hospitality, and may I offer hospitality to friends, neighbors, and strangers without grumbling. For I know You are just as interested in the attitude of the gift being administered as You are in the gift itself. May I extend Your generosity to those around me.

In Jesus' Name, Amen.

When I'm Battling Shame

KEY SCRIPTURE:

For the Scripture says, "Whoever believes
on Him will not be put to shame."
ROMANS 10:11

Father,

I thank You that when I am obedient to Your Word, I am conformed to the image of Christ. When I read and study Your Word, I am made holy by Your truth. Help me become in practice what I already am in position. Let the mirror of Your Word reflect truth to me, exposing and cleansing my thoughts, motives, and actions. Through this pain and confrontation, change me from glory to glory until I look and act more like Jesus.

You have begun a good work in me, and I know You will finish that work. There's no mistake I can make that would prevent You from finishing it. May my character match the fruit of the Holy Spirit now. Sanctify me; cleanse me by the power of Your Word, and bring holiness into my life.

In Jesus' Name, Amen.

PRAYER FOR...

When I
Need Peace
in My Home

KEY SCRIPTURE:

By wisdom a house is built, and through understanding
it is established; through knowledge its rooms are
filled with rare and beautiful treasures.
PROVERBS 24:3-4, NIV

Dear Lord,

What a blessing it is to be part of a home and part of a family. Thank You for this wonderful gift. Help me assimilate Your Holy Scriptures into my mind and heart and live them out every day in my home. I pray for godliness and peace to increase within each heart and each relationship. And may Your wisdom and guidance bring peace. Give me knowledge so that harmony and blessing are the rare and beautiful treasures that fill my home.

I know that Your principles work, and I thank You that I am not left in this world to follow the advice of humanism or the world's methods. Instead, I have Your Word. Let the environment of my home encourage direction, purpose, faith, and dedication. And give me understanding so that I can build a home that testifies to those around me of Your goodness.

In Jesus' Name, Amen.

PRAYER FOR...

When My
Heart Is Heavy

KEY SCRIPTURE:

So do not fear, for I am with you; do not be dismayed,
for I am your God. I will strengthen you and help you;
I will uphold you with my righteous right hand.
ISAIAH 41:10, NIV

Heavenly Father,

Thank You for drawing close to those who are brokenhearted. Thank You for drawing close to me when I am brokenhearted. The challenge of my circumstances and the anxieties of daily life weigh me down.

Lord, I know that nothing comes from the wisdom of the world but havoc, total disintegration, and destruction, so please give me the courage to get my direction and strength from You. The heaviness of my heart is a burden I cannot lift. But You say that You are the Lord who daily bears my burdens, and You save me when I feel troubled.

I choose not to fear because I believe You are with me. Help me see Your right hand of favor, ready to bless me here and now. Let me rest in the shadow of Your wings, safe from all oppression and worry.

In Christ's Name, Amen.

When I Receive God's Correction

KEY SCRIPTURE:

Endure hardship as discipline; God is treating you as his
children. For what children are not disciplined by their father?
HEBREWS 12:7, NIV

Heavenly Father,

I know You take my discipline seriously because it proves Your love for me. You don't correct me out of anger or disappointment; instead, You instruct me in the way I should go. Structure my life in such a way that I live according to the precepts You have set before me.

Thank You that You are not punitive; You are preventative. You don't want to penalize me. You want to instruct and correct me. Help me submit to Your correction. Thank You that You reach out Your mighty hand and give me boundaries to prevent me from harm and destruction.

Help me see Your Word and commands as guardrails, keeping me from danger. May I clearly understand the parameters of Your Word, and may I continually commit and agree to them.

In Jesus' mighty Name, Amen.

When God
Feels Far Away

KEY SCRIPTURE:

Why, Lord, do you stand far off? Why do you hide yourself in times of trouble?... But you, God, see the trouble of the afflicted; you consider their grief and take it in hand.
PSALM 10:1, 14, NIV

Dear Lord,

I am suffering, so why aren't You coming to help? It's difficult to get my thoughts together. I think of the former times that seem so far away—those seasons when You took care of me and I felt Your friendship. I cry to You, but it seems I get no answers. My voice of joy and gladness has turned into mourning. Now I'm sitting on the ash heap.

But I believe You are sitting here with me. Your Spirit is here to comfort me. Your Word tells me that You see beauty in ashes.

Help me believe the truth of Your presence, even when I cannot see or feel Your nearness. You will never leave me and never forsake me. Help me trust Your Word above my own imagination.

In the name of Emmanuel, Amen.

When It Seems God Is Silent

KEY SCRIPTURE:

I go forward, but He is not there, and backward,
but I cannot perceive Him; when He works on the
left hand, I cannot behold Him; when He turns to the
right hand, I cannot see Him. But He knows the way that
I take; when He has tested me, I shall come forth as gold.
JOB 23:8-10

Father,

Thank You for Your Word that guides me when You seem silent. When You do not seem to be answering, I can lose perspective. I can overreact and jump to the wrong conclusions. Help me not lose sound judgment as I walk through this desert. I know that You refresh my soul, even when the heavens seem silent.

I don't want a distorted view of You, so help me not to worry but instead remember that You know the way that I take. May I be still and wait patiently for You. For I know that those who wait upon You will not be disappointed.

In Jesus' Name, Amen.

When I've Received Bad News

KEY SCRIPTURE:

Though He slay me, yet will I trust Him.
JOB 13:15

Lord God,

You understood Job's frailty and the extreme loss that he experienced. And I know that You understand mine as well. Even when I am confronted with terrible news, disaster, and loss, thank You for Your presence and promise to be with me. Help me accept that life and people are not always fair.

But I know You are just and You never allow anything to happen in my life for which You do not have a purpose. Thank You that I am Your child, and despite this difficult moment, I will never lose Your favor. Though I may struggle and wrestle with questions in the confusion of this moment, may the flame of my faith never be extinguished.

I choose to trust You until the end. I choose to trust You even though I don't understand. And I choose to trust You even if I never understand because I believe You are good.

In Jesus' Name, Amen.

PRAYER FOR...

When I'm Feeling Grateful for Blessings

KEY SCRIPTURE:

*Be filled with the Spirit, speaking to one another in psalms
and hymns and spiritual songs, singing and making melody
in your heart to the Lord, giving thanks always for all
things to God the Father in the name of our Lord Jesus
Christ, submitting to one another in the fear of God.*
EPHESIANS 5:18-21

Father,

I am surrounded by Your blessings. I see them in my home. I see
them in my community. I see them in my work and my purpose.
Your blessings are all around me. For the goodness You've provided,
I give You thanks. For the gift of life, I praise You. For the sunrise
and new mercies, for breath and opportunity, I thank You. I even
want to thank You for the difficulties. In everything, You teach me
to thank You.

I'm kneeling in Your presence right now with the key of
thanksgiving. I know that being thankful is evidence that Your Holy
Spirit fills my life. First thing in the morning, I thank You. During a
break, I praise You. At lunch, I give You thanks, and at dinner, I offer
gratitude. In the evening before bed, I praise You. Throughout the
day, Your praise will be on my lips. For You have been good to me.

I thank You in Jesus' Name, Amen.

When I Need Comfort in Grief

KEY SCRIPTURE:

All praise to God, the Father of our Lord Jesus Christ. God is our merciful Father and the source of all comfort. He comforts us in all our troubles so that we can comfort others. When they are troubled, we will be able to give them the same comfort God has given us. For the more we suffer for Christ, the more God will shower us with his comfort through Christ.
2 CORINTHIANS 1:3-5, NLT

Father,

I cannot bear this grief alone. This loss is indescribable, and I'm not sure how to hope again. I cannot find any reason why You allowed this tragedy to happen to me. But I know that no one is beyond the reach of Your love. I know You are acquainted with grief—a Man of Sorrows. So I come to the God of all comfort to receive the comfort only You can give.

Fill me with the truth of Your Word and bless me with Your healing touch. Draw me close to You, and never let me go. I thank You for walking with me through the valley of the shadow of death. Let Your goodness and love follow me through this grief. Uphold me today and always.

In Jesus' mighty Name, Amen.

When I'm in Pain

KEY SCRIPTURE:

I would have lost heart, unless I had believed that I would see the goodness of the Lord in the land of the living. Wait on the Lord; be of good courage, and He shall strengthen your heart; wait, I say, on the Lord!
PSALM 27:13-14

Father,

I'm experiencing physical pain and emotional and spiritual anguish. Both my body and spirit are breaking. It seems like the only thing I know is the pain of my own life. My misery confounds me. This dark night of the soul distorts my thinking. Help me, Lord, to stand strong in this test. Energize my prayers, for I know You understand my pain and offer me mercy.

I've stood with You on mountaintops, but now I need You in the valley. I'm coming boldly before You to receive all You are ready to give. Help me not to despair but to trust in You through the pain. Lift my low spirit and restore my body and my mind so that I might serve You in the land of the living. I am grateful for times of good health, but if this pain leads me to You, help me be grateful for it too.

In Jesus' Name, Amen.

PRAYER FOR…

When I Need
Rest for My Soul

KEY SCRIPTURE:

Truly my soul finds rest in God; my salvation comes from him.
PSALM 62:1, NIV

Heavenly Father,

I feel tired in my body and in my mind. But I am also weary in my soul. You know all the circumstances in my life, which means You understand everything I am experiencing right now. You understand how circumstances have affected me better than I understand myself.

For that reason, please have mercy on me, Lord God. I picture my soul as a fallow field, ready for renewal, and I ask that You please help me find rest. I want to experience contentment and fulfillment, and I know that only comes through staying close to You. So here I am. Restore my soul, and help me develop rhythms of rest.

Thank You that You invite anyone who is burdened or weary to come to You and You promise rest. Your Word declares that blessing belongs to the one who knows You and walks in the light from Your face. May that be true of me right now!

In Christ's Name, Amen.

When I Need Restoration

KEY SCRIPTURE:

Blessed is the one whose transgressions are forgiven, whose sins are covered. Blessed is the one whose sin the Lord does not count against them and in whose spirit is no deceit. When I kept silent, my bones wasted away through my groaning all day long. For day and night your hand was heavy on me; my strength was sapped as in the heat of summer. Then I acknowledged my sin to you and did not cover up my iniquity. I said, "I will confess my transgressions to the Lord." And you forgave the guilt of my sin.
PSALM 32:1-5, NIV

Father,

My transgressions are forgiven, and my sins are covered. Thank You that I don't need to pay over and over and over again for what I have done. Let Your mercy be like the tide washing away footprints. Lord, clear my past and make space for new beginnings. I know that restoration is found in You.

I confess the error of my ways to You and pray to You now—I cannot keep silent anymore. Though the consequences of my actions may not be eliminated immediately, I know that You bless me with forgiveness and do not count my sin against me. And for those affected by my choices, I pray for Your protection, healing, and blessing upon them.

In Jesus' Name, Amen.

When I'm Physically Exhausted

KEY SCRIPTURE:

It is good to give thanks to the Lord, and to sing praises to Your name, O Most High; to declare Your lovingkindness in the morning, and Your faithfulness every night.
PSALM 92:1-2

Father,

Thank You that Your mercy is new in the morning. When the race of life is wearing me down, help me remember to stop and offer a moment of thanks. I am exhausted; the days' demands pull from every direction—but I can still lift my head. When I do that, I can experience Your lovingkindness in the morning and Your faithfulness at night.

Like a river replenishing a dry streambed, may Your life wash over my depleted soul. Help me rest in You, finding complete peace and energy again. Renew my strength so that I can run and not grow weary. Help me walk and not faint.

I love You and thank You in Jesus' Name, Amen.

When I Fear Natural Disasters

KEY SCRIPTURE:

Surely the righteous will never be shaken; they will
be remembered forever. They will have no fear of bad
news; their hearts are steadfast, trusting in the Lord.
Their hearts are secure, they will have no fear.
PSALM 112:6-8, NIV

Dear Lord,

Creation seems to be groaning as in the pains of childbirth. Each time I look at the news it seems another disaster has overtaken people. But You are the Lord and there is no other. So when I feel anxious, help me to pray and sing hymns to You. I don't have the assurance that a disaster won't occur, but I do have Your promises that You are my protector and that my life is in Your hands.

You said the righteous will never be shaken and that I don't need to fear bad news. May my heart be steadfast, trusting in You.

Help me to quit studying the problems and start studying the promises. By the power of the Holy Spirit, may I be thankful to You, Almighty God, no matter what comes. I worship You today, and where worship is, worry cannot remain.

In Jesus' Name, Amen.

When I Don't Feel Accepted

KEY SCRIPTURE:

Hear my voice when I call, Lord; be merciful to me and answer me. My heart says of you, "Seek his face!" Your face, Lord, I will seek. Do not hide your face from me, do not turn your servant away in anger; you have been my helper. Do not reject me or forsake me, God my Savior. Though my father and mother forsake me, the Lord will receive me.
PSALM 27:7-10, NIV

Heavenly Father,

I'm having a hard time feeling accepted. I feel distant and separated from those I love. But I know that You accept me. I know that You will not reject me or forsake me. So today I pray that You will help me receive Your embrace. Help me believe that You have adopted me as Your beloved child because You wanted me.

I acknowledge my need and thank You for Your stamp of approval. You have been my safe refuge, and I seek You now. Thank You for always offering me Your eternal blessing.

In Jesus' Name, Amen.

When I Fear Making the Wrong Decision

KEY SCRIPTURE:

Your word is a lamp to my feet and a light to my path.
PSALM 119:105

Dear Heavenly Father,

Your Word guides me; it's my light in a dark place. Thank You for illuminating my way, even when I'm afraid I'll miss the way. I feel paralyzed by fear and can't see what's ahead. Help me understand that faith isn't about perfection but about following Your direction.

I pray that when I close my eyes, You will help me remember and reflect on all that You have done for me. You have rescued me from the grasp of sin and death. I remember Your forgiveness, and it awakens a deep well of gratitude in my heart.

Thank You that even when I falter, You never give up on me. You guide and direct me in each decision I make. So I receive Your presence and encouragement now and release my fear to You.

In Christ's Name, Amen.

When I Worry About the Future

KEY SCRIPTURE:

For to us a child is born, to us a son is given, and the government will be on his shoulders. And he will be called Wonderful Counselor, Mighty God, Everlasting Father, Prince of Peace. Of the greatness of his government and peace there will be no end. He will reign on David's throne and over his kingdom, establishing and upholding it with justice and righteousness from that time on and forever. The zeal of the Lord Almighty will accomplish this.
ISAIAH 9:6-7, NIV

Father,

You reign supreme over the heavens and the earth. When every headline is like a storm gathering on the horizon and it seems like there is chaos ahead, I know You create peace without end. Today I declare my hope and confidence that You reign in the squall of my soul. The government rests on Your shoulders, and today I come to the Wonderful Counselor, the Mighty God, and my Everlasting Father.

Help me not fear what the future holds, for You are steadfast and true. Help me take heart in the gift of the reigning Lord Jesus Christ. Let His everlasting rule of peace reign on earth and in me. In this moment I welcome the greatness of Jesus' governing in my life, and I release my fear to You.

In Christ's Name, Amen.

PRAYER FOR…

When I Am Grieving the Loss of a Loved One

KEY SCRIPTURE:

Through the Lord's mercies we are not consumed,
because His compassions fail not. They are new
every morning; great is Your faithfulness.
LAMENTATIONS 3:22-23

Heavenly Father,

I am experiencing the sting of death, and it hurts. Please remind me of Your mercy and compassion for me.

I thank You for preserving my faith through the ups and downs of life. Whatever I need, whenever I need it, You are there with the special medicine of Your mercy. And now, I need Your comfort. This loss is a heavy burden; share it with me. Give me Your yoke so we can take each step forward together.

In this time of grief, Your Word says that You are quick to keep me from stumbling. Lord, keep me from losing my way, from turning away from the faith and going down a detour. I know that to walk with You is to walk in safety even in the most dangerous and slippery times.

Comfort me and keep me from stumbling. Keep me on the high road, doing the things I need to do without forgetting who I am and what I am called to do. Hold on to me today.

In Jesus' Name, Amen.

When I'm Starting a New Job

KEY SCRIPTURE:

Now to Him who is able to do exceedingly abundantly
above all that we ask or think, according to the power
that works in us, to Him be glory in the church by Christ
Jesus to all generations, forever and ever. Amen.
EPHESIANS 3:20-21

Lord,

I thank You and praise You for opening a new door for me. As I learn to carry out this work, give me wisdom to always do so according to Your principles. If I am tempted or pressured to violate those principles, help me walk by faith and declare that I have higher orders.

I know You are able to do more than I can ask or imagine. Bless me with wisdom and understanding as I begin this new job. Help me diligently work in my responsibilities and conduct myself as unto the Lord. May I walk by faith, obedient to what You tell me in Your Word, recognizing Your leading and direction in this new endeavor. Help me see Your power at work in me, living every day of my life growing more and more like Christ and glorifying You in all that I do.

In Jesus' Name, Amen.

When I Need to Take a Step of Faith

KEY SCRIPTURE:

By faith Abraham obeyed when he was called to go out to the place which he would receive as an inheritance. And he went out, not knowing where he was going. By faith he dwelt in the land of promise as in a foreign country, dwelling in tents with Isaac and Jacob, the heirs with him of the same promise; for he waited for the city which has foundations, whose builder and maker is God.
HEBREWS 11:8-10

Father,

You have called me to walk by faith. I'm not putting my trust in a warm and fuzzy feeling about You. You have asked me to put my trust in the revelation that You have given me and the revelation that You will give me in the future.

I'm not taking a partial step of obedience; I am fully committing to this calling. And when I'm out here, feeling a little like I'm on the edge, please come along and confirm that I have done the right thing.

Lord, I know that trusting always involves waiting, so I take this step and trust that You will build my faith through this journey. Let it be more adventurous than I have ever dreamed—for I know You will be faithful to me.

In Jesus' mighty Name, Amen.

When I Need Spiritual Focus

KEY SCRIPTURE:

Blessed is the man… [whose] delight is in the law of the Lord, and in His law he meditates day and night. He shall be like a tree planted by the rivers of water, that brings forth its fruit in its season, whose leaf also shall not wither; and whatever he does shall prosper.
PSALM 1:1-3

Heavenly Father,

I thank You for Your Word, and I'm grateful that You are present with me. I sense that You are doing something in my life, and I thank You. Sometimes it's difficult to read Your Word, especially when I don't understand it. Help me make it a part of my life each day. Give me a renewed hunger for the daily bread of Your Word. Help me to see what it says and understand what it means.

I want You to know I'm willing to do whatever You tell me because I want to do Your will. I want to know Your purpose. I'm excited about the potential of Your calling on my life, and I know I need Your Word to complete the tasks You've placed in front of me.

I realize I'm not sufficient for these things, but I'm also grateful that when I have You on my side, I'm always in the majority. You can do what no man can do, so help me commit to Your Word and Your purpose.

In Jesus' Name, Amen.

Personal Prayers

Continue earnestly in prayer,
being vigilant in it with thanksgiving.

COLOSSIANS 4:2

PRAYER REQUESTS

———

ANSWERED PRAYERS

_____

_____

_____

_____

_____

_____

_____

_____

_____

_____

_____

_____

_____

_____

_____

_____

_____

_____

PRAYER REQUESTS

———

_____

_____

_____

_____

_____

_____

_____

_____

_____

_____

_____

_____

_____

_____

ANSWERED PRAYERS

———

PRAYER REQUESTS

———

_____

_____

_____

_____

_____

_____

_____

_____

_____

_____

_____

_____

ANSWERED PRAYERS

STAY CONNECTED TO
DR. DAVID JEREMIAH

Take advantage of three great ways to let Dr. Jeremiah
give you spiritual direction every day!

TURNING POINTS MAGAZINE & DEVOTIONAL

Have Dr. David Jeremiah's monthly magazine delivered
directly to your home. Each issue includes:

- A thematic study focus
- Relevant articles
- Daily devotional readings
- Bible study resource offers
- Radio & television information

Request *Turning Points* magazine today!

(800) 947-1993

DavidJeremiah.org/Magazine

DAILY TURNING POINT E-DEVOTIONAL

Find words of inspiration and spiritual motivation
in your inbox every morning. Each e-devotional from
David Jeremiah will strengthen your walk with God
and encourage you to live with authentic faith.

Sign up for your free e-devotional today!

DavidJeremiah.org/Devo

TURNING POINT MOBILE APP

Access Dr. David Jeremiah's video teachings, audio ser-
mons, and more… whenever and wherever you are.

Download the free app today!

DavidJeremiah.org/App